FEAR · LOVE ·
LOVE · FEAR
FEAR · LOVE
FEAR · LOVE ·
FEAR · LOVE ·
LOVE ·
LOVE ·
LOVE · FEAR · LOVE
FEAR · LOVE
FEAR ·
LOVE · FEAR

Toltec Prophecies
of
Don Miguel Ruiz

Also by don Miguel Ruiz and
Mary Carroll Nelson:

BEYOND FEAR

A Toltec Guide to Freedom and Love

Also by don Miguel Ruiz:

THE FOUR AGREEMENTS

A Practical Guide to Personal Freedom

THE MASTERY OF LOVE

A Practical Guide to the Art of Relationship

PRAYERS

A Communion with Our Creator

TOLTEC PROPHECIES
OF
DON MIGUEL RUIZ

Mary Carroll Nelson

COUNCIL OAK BOOKS

Tulsa / San Francisco

Book design: Mary Beth Salmon
Cover photo and illustrations: ©2003 by Linda Stilley

Printed in Canada
ISBN 1-57178-134-X

Council Oak Books
2105 E 15th Street, Suite B
Tulsa, OK 74104
800.247.8850

www.counciloakbooks.com

4 3 2 1   06 05 04 03

Awake, the sky is reddening
The dawn is breaking
The flame-colored pheasants
are singing
The butterflies take wing.

He has awakened.
He has become a god.

From the rites of death at
Teotihuacan

CONTENTS

Foreword

I believe that each person we meet is, potentially, an agent of our future. I first met don Miguel Ruiz in the early 1990s, in Santa Fe, New Mexico, where he was living. My purpose in arranging to meet him grew from a discovery I had made that certain artists and others who are healers and shamans have a similar type of creativity. Through interviews, I met people who had experienced an abrupt, jolting change in their lives that led them to new insights. They then created an altruistic way to share their wisdom with others. I called such wise people *Artists of the Spirit* and was writing a book with that title. When I heard about Miguel from a fellow artist, I knew that I was meant to interview him.

As I arrived to interview Miguel, he was about to give a healing treatment to a woman who suffered severely from arthritis and he allowed me to observe the session. I saw this small dark man, with liquid brown eyes, totally focused on conveying through massage an energy that was visibly affecting his client. She had been desperate to have the treatment before leaving on an extended trip. I was moved by her evident relief and also by what seemed to be the trance-like state of her healer.

Just after his client left, vastly restored, Miguel and I visited. He had a feeling that someone would appear who would write about him, and here I was. Over the brief space of a half hour, in which he sat very close and held my hand, Miguel must have decided that I am not a threatening person, and so began our five year interaction. Miguel's work was expanding and he traveled frequently. Our interviews and reviews of what I had written were widely spaced to fit his schedule. Just as we were finishing the biographical chapter for *Artists of the Spirit,* he asked me if I would consider writing a book of his teachings. I agreed with the proviso that I would be an observer, not an apprentice. My objectivity was, I believe, what he preferred. And I spent several years on his teachings, as well as traveling with him on two tours of Teotihuacan, down the mile-long ancient Avenue of the Dead, learning the purpose of the pyramids from Miguel. After years of collaboration, our book, *Beyond Fear,* was published in 1997.

I absorbed a considerable amount of Toltec lore during my many talks with Miguel. I am especially drawn to the idea that human beings are not only astoundingly creative but also that with our fertile minds and varied emotions, we are actually dreaming this world, a world that is wonderful, beautiful and inspiring but, at the same time, is a nightmare that spawns hatred, illness, calamities in our environment, and cruelty to others.

Miguel teaches that we have the power to eliminate the nightmare by controlling our dream. He believes we are headed toward an awakening in consciousness and recognition of our creative power. His prophecies bring hope. They place the future in our hands and they replace the excuses of sophisticated arguments, academic reasoning, and cynical pessimism with a set of basic premises that substantiate the perfection of our creation. We came into life with all the abilities we need to create Heaven on Earth. Those three words, often repeated in our conversations, remain with me. I think about them when I move through my day. Miguel stresses that it is not so important what happens to us as it is what happens through us. Such a lesson justifies the reflection this book may inspire within you. I believe many readers will be uplifted by don Miguel's *Toltec Prophecies* and the clarity of his understanding of Toltec wisdom.

About the prophecies

Don Miguel Ruiz bases his teaching on the primary Toltec concept that everything that exists is one living being. This one living being is everything we can perceive and everything we cannot. *This one living being is the only one who really exists. All else, including humanity, is an emanation of this great and wonderful being.*

In modern science, everything that exists in the world is energy. Light is energy, and everything, at its root, is light. In the Toltec tradition, the information carried by light is called *the silent knowledge,* and all of us are vessels of the light. The primary source of all information is at the center of the universe. In our region of the universe, the source is at the center of the Milky Way, our own galaxy. Locally, our source is the sun.

The first part of this book describes aspects that will help us understand the prophecies. We will learn about the anatomy of the living being, how reality is created and how we can transcend the nightmare of hell on earth. The second part is devoted to the Toltec prophecies themselves—which are all coming true right now, don Miguel tells us, because the world's dream is changing.

At the center of don Miguel's spiritual knowledge and practice is helping others replace fear with love. We are all inculcated with fear which lies at the root of the reality we perceive around us, causing disease, war, and alienation from the joy that is our birthright.

In the West we have lived with the foreboding of an inevitable cataclysmic Armageddon which we feel helpless to prevent. We are vulnerable to a pervasive fear. Fear is the cause of the nightmare that dominates our planet.

Don Ruiz provides a different, far older prophecy of a future entirely of our own making. We have the power, he tells us, to replace fear with a new dream of Heaven on Earth. The solution to the survival of the human race rests with our intention. We can focus our intention to create the vibrant future we desire, individually and collectively. The *Toltec Prophecies* come at a pivotal point in human consciousness when many people around the Earth are awakening to an expanded awareness of their own potential. Don Miguel Ruiz is an important teacher for our time.

—Mary Carroll Nelson, 2003

TOLTEC WISDOM

I am not teaching anything. I am just reminding others of what they remember that they know. The knowledge I bear is not my own. It is in everyone.

—don Miguel Ruiz

The Sixth Sun

On January 11, 1992, the Sixth Sun rose, the color of the sunlight changed, the vibration of the sunlight became faster and gentler, and we began metabolizing a different quality of energy. It is difficult to test this new light energy in a laboratory because, through science, we do not yet understand light as a living being. Light is basically undetectable by our limited science now, but in time we will prove that it is a living biological being with intelligence and the source of our own intelligence.

The light of the Sixth Sun is now intensifying human creativity, imagination and intelligence. The **Toltec Prophecies** will help us understand how this light change will affect humanity, and how we can adapt to the changes this amazing new light will spark.

ONE UNIVERSAL BEING

Humans are multidimensional in matter, in mind, and in soul, but we are *unidimensional* in spirit. Because we are multidimensional living beings, each of us can perceive thousands of things individually. Because we are unidimensional in spirit, we collectively perceive thousands of things simultaneously.

In matter we find that our bodies are made by billions and billions of tiny living beings that we call cells. Every cell is an individual that we can take out of our bodies and put in the laboratory where it will stay alive. At the same time, it will continue to be a part of our body. A liver cell has no awareness that it is part of a whole being. It does not know that, together with the other cells in the liver, brain, heart, bones and all the cells throughout the body, it helps to form this single living human being.

All humans together form one living being which is an organ of Planet Earth. Each human is to the earth what a single cell is to a human body. Cells live and die continuously in our bodies just as we humans are born, mature, and die. This constant replenishment of humans keeps the human organ of the earth alive. Likewise, on different time scales, this same process of physical life giving way to physical death occurs throughout the universe.

Life on earth and beyond is divided into organs. A single human being is one part of the organ called humanity. The totality of all humans forms one organ of Planet Earth which, like a human body, is itself alive and has its own metabolism. There are many organs in this beautiful living being: the atmosphere,

being

the oceans, and the forests each form an organ. All the animals are an organ. And, although we are often unaware, we humans communicate with the other organs in the same way that the liver communicates with the heart and with the brain.

Every planet is an organ of the one living being. Together, the sun and all the planets are one being. Each unit from an electron to a galaxy is a single being united with larger beings.

Planet Earth is an organ of the solar system with the sun at the center and all the planets, moons, and other satellites in orbit around the sun. The solar system too is a single living being ruled by the sun, and is, at the same time, only a small piece of the gigantic being that we call the universe.

A single atom with its electrons in orbit around its nucleus forms another solar system, making the atoms and solar system analogous. Our bodies are composed of billions of atoms, each a miniature solar system. In the universe there are billions of stars, each a living being—but together they form just one living being. The Toltecs understood these analogies and similarities which were reflected in different realities throughout the universe.

Who are we? Where did we come from?

One small human body is a single piece of a chain within the huge biological machine that is the universe. Just as an atom within a human body is in constant communication with the brain, this chain communicates with everything else that exists in the whole universe. We are everything that is.

In the material perspective we are everything our eyes and ears perceive. But, we are not simply matter. We are also what we feel; anger, jealousy, sadness, happiness, and love. These emotions of human life provide evidence of another dimension of energy. We call these emotions *ethereal energy*. Material energy is that which is detectable and proved by scientific methods. Ethereal energy cannot be proved within the limits of mainstream science. We cannot prove that hate or love exists, but we experience their effects. Emotional energy is ethereal energy.

Energy is alive, just as everything else that exists is alive. Ethereal energy, itself a living being, includes our emotions—which are alive. Our thinking is also alive. All of our thoughts and feelings are alive, and they are us. Our minds are creating billions of emotions, and, in the same way that our cells create our bodies, our emotions create our minds. Our minds are made of ethereal energy.

Our minds are made by our emotions. Everything the mind perceives has an emotional component. When light of varying frequencies strikes material objects, it is reflected in our eyes. The brain translates these light images of material energy into matter, and what the mind creates we perceive as reality. Actually, this reality is a dream. We dream twenty-four hours a day, whether the brain is awake or asleep.

The brain can change energy in both directions. It has the capacity to transform material energy into ethereal energy. We create ideas and ideas are ethereal energy. When the brain converts ethereal energy into words and writing, we manifest into the material world what we are dreaming in our mind. The mind creates imagination and the imagination dreams. The old ways of dreaming reality lead us into suffering and emotional pain. This is true of all of us. We suffer when we are afraid of losing what we are and what we have.

Change can begin

with a single mind.

In the Toltec tradition our efforts are directed toward raising our personal awareness away from the fear-driven old dream of the planet to a new dream of heaven on earth. However, the old dream is thousands of years old and is deeply entrenched in the minds of all humans. The dream is a living being. It is an archangel that came from the sun. The old dream believes itself to be real and is afraid to die. It tries to protect its existence by creating fear in the human mind.

Spirit is pushing us to change the dream. When we entered the Sixth Sun, it gave us the opportunity to make this change in the dream. More than an opportunity, it was a command from the sun telling us it has to happen.

DREAMING MIND

The function of our mind is to dream twenty-four hours a day. Awake or asleep, we dream with our mind, not with our brain. Yet, the brain knows that the mind is dreaming.

The waking dream has a material structure. In sleep, the dream also seems to have a structure. While awake, our mind is affected by cycles of energy through the day as the light changes, and this rhythm gives the mind a notion of time and space. During sleep, we do not perceive energy from outside our-selves, but the mind dreams images including an image of our own body. We can talk, see and even fly in a dream. We do not notice that we are asleep when we are dreaming.

Something makes the connection between the inner dream and the outer dream. That something is *reason*. Reason is the part of the mind that tries to qualify and understand everything. Reason wants to say, this is real and this is unreal. Reason gives us the illusion that the dream is real as long as the dream has the material framework we perceive as reality. We do not notice that we are interpreting reality according to the dream we are in at the moment.

All humans together form an organ of the earth, but this organ exists in a different dimension from that of our bodies. Our bodies are a part of the mate-rial dimension which we can touch. Our minds exist in the ethereal dimension of thoughts and feelings. In the same way that our thoughts and minds create an individual mind, all minds together create the mind of the Planet Earth, and that mind is dreaming, too.

dream

This collective dream includes the dreams of the family, the dreams of the community, of the city, of the state, of the country, of the whole continent, and finally the dream of the whole planet.

At each level of dreaming, there are distinct differences in the dream. For example, if we visit another country, we will find that its dream is different from that of our own country, and it is alive. The dream in China is different from the one in Persia, but there is something in common in the dreams. People everywhere suffer. People struggle. In their interactions, people everywhere spread poison. This is an ethereal poison, not a physical one, but the poison still affects the physical body. The poisons we call anger, hate, sadness, jealousy, shyness, all come from the same ethereal energy that controls the dream of the planet—and this is fear.

Fear is the big demon, the big devil in the dream of the planet. Our interactions with each other are based on fear, human to human, society to society, nation to nation. The way we dream fear is self-destructive. We are destroying ourselves as individuals and as a society.

No matter where we go, we will find that people have a judge and a victim in their minds. They all find guilt in themselves and in other people. When we feel guilty, we have a need to be punished. When others are guilty, we need to punish them. This is a function of fear.

The victim is that part of the mind that says, "Poor me. I'm not good enough. I'm not strong enough. I'm not intelligent enough. How can I survive? Why should I try? I'm just a human." So, every step is fearful. That is the way humans have learned to dream. This is a function of fear.

We live in the nightmare of hell. The fears in one human mind become bigger when they are projected outside. Our community is a society that dreams of fear, injustice, and punishment. Our teenagers are killing each other, and we find hatred in all parts of the world. Even our entertainment is studded with violence.

The nightmare of hell is a disease of the human mind. The whole world is a hospital.

Heaven is the exact opposite of hell. It is a place of joy, love, peace, communion and understanding with neither a judge nor a victim. In heaven there is clarity. We know what we are. We no longer blame ourselves or others. A dream is a living being. Whether in heaven or hell, we create the dream and the dream creates our lives. But we are free to leave the nightmare and dream heaven anytime.

The Dream of the Planet, held by all of us, is the same. When we rise out of the Dream of the Planet and out of our own dream, we find that what we have thought of as truth is nothing but information in our mind and that can easily be changed. We resist change because we are afraid. Fear controls our life. Fear controls the nightmare of hell.

From outside the planet, we can see that the evolution of the whole human race is akin to the life of a single living being who is born, grows and reproduces, and will transform. Everything is indestructible really. It does not die. It transforms.

The progress of evolution has a certain logic. The living being of all humans combined will undergo changes in the same way that a single human changes.

The *Toltec Prophecies* are about changing the dream and the Sixth Sun has come to speed the process.

What we see is nothing but light reflecting from objects. Perception is a miracle that demonstrates our power to create the outside reality. We think we perceive the natural world, but we actually create it in our mind and brain.

The real core of a human being is a personal ray of light in connection with the sun. Whatever happens in the single human is known by the sun through this light. Any change occurring in a single human affects the sun and its response affects the rest of humanity. This is the process of human evolution.

WE ARE THE LIGHT

Changing the dream involves coming to the light, releasing the light, seeing the light from many directions.

Our body is light, but it is condensed light. Our mind is light. Our soul is light in different manifestations. Light perceives light in any of the dimensions. This is why we can perceive with the eyes, but we also can perceive with the mind, with the soul, and with the spirit.

What is the spirit? I call it intent. Intent, spirit, God...these are names for the same energy. A property of intent energy is that it makes possible any change, any transformation. God is intent. God is spirit. God is God. God is light. God is the real you. God is the real me.

Energy or light is the first manifestation of intent, or the first manifestation of God, or of the spirit. Everything is alive because of God, because of you. You are not your body. You are not your cells. You are not your mind. You are not your soul. You are light. You are life. Your essence is light and light is everywhere.

Light is a living being. There are billions of different vibrations of light. Light carries all the information for any kind of life on Planet Earth. Mother Earth transforms the information in the light from the Father Sun to create life. The DNA in each of our cells is a ray from the sun condensed into matter by Mother Earth.

The information carried by the light is known as the *silent knowledge*. The silent knowledge is

light

stored and passed on in DNA; therefore our bodies contain the codes.

All knowledge that exists is in the light. Light is the way stars communicate from one to the other, just as light is the way one atom communicates with another atom.

Each human has a frequency of light, which is always connected to the sun, like a river to earth. If we shift our focus, it is possible to see that the river of light as something solid in the same way that we see a human hand as something solid. If we shift our focus to a smaller, swifter time and space, we no longer see the human hand as solid. Instead we can see all the atoms, all the electrons as a field of energy that is moving and not solid. The river of light, like any river, is flowing. It is constantly moving and changing.

We are all connected to the same sun. Whatever happens anywhere in the universe will be known by the whole universe because the communication is instantaneous. In our material point of view, the speed of light is 186,000 miles per second, which we think is probably the fastest speed possible, but actually there is a quality of light that is thousands of times faster than our ability to measure it. It is this quality that allows for instant communication across the universe and to all the organs of the universe.

What we see is nothing but light reflecting from objects. Reflected light gives the objects apparent form. We have agreed to accept our visual perceptions of reality as the truth, but this truth derives from an agreement or consensus in which we are a partner. Perception is a miracle that demonstrates our power to create the outside reality. We perceive the natural world, but we actually created it in our mind and brain.

As soon as we interpret what we are seeing, we find that each of us makes a different interpretation of reality because each of us dreams a different dream. Each of us has our own dream based on what we have agreed to believe.

The real core of a human being is a personal ray of light in connection with the sun. Whatever happens in the single human is known by the sun through this light. Any change occurring in a single human affects the sun and its response affects the rest of humanity.

Once we find our personal ray of light, we can shift our point of view to the sun and see the human race all at once. I teach my apprentices to find that ray of light connecting them to the sun. When they can do this, the silent knowledge enters their minds and they just know, without thought or fear. Humans who can do this are prophets who point the way for others.

Ask to die to the old

dream of the planet.

Prepare to leave hell.

Begin to imagine

heaven on earth.

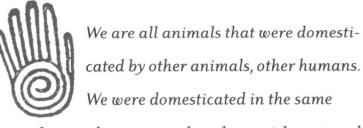 *We are all animals that were domesticated by other animals, other humans. We were domesticated in the same way that we domesticate dogs, by punishment and reward. We domesticate our children the way we were domesticated. We are afraid to be punished and we are afraid not to get the reward.*

HUMAN DOMESTICATION

Imagine a thousand new computers exactly alike, each completely blank, without information. As soon as we put information into these computers, each will be different.

Our minds are biological machines that resemble computers. There is different information in every human being according to each person's experience. Each one has learned differently from parents, society, school and religion. The information that we put into our computer is what tells us how to interpret what we perceive.

Each human computer has a name, but a name is only an agreement we have made. I am not really a human being named Miguel Ruiz. You are not a human being either. We just agree that we are humans. Everything that we put into our computers is an agreement. It is not necessarily good or bad, right or wrong. It is just information. According to that information, we perceive the world and call it reality. This information is the source of our limitations. We create images about ourselves and about everything else. We then want to believe in those images. The process of putting the information into the computer is the Domestication.

We are all animals that were domesticated by other animals, other humans. We were domesticated in the same way that we domesticate dogs, by punishment and reward. We domesticate our children the way we were domesticated. We are afraid to be punished and afraid not to get the reward. We create images of ourselves designed to please others. We belief

want to be good enough to please mom and dad, the teacher, society, the church and God. Our behavior depends upon the image we have created about ourselves, with all those limitations. What others think about us is very important to us. We guide our lives with reference to others' opinions. We try to please everybody else, rather than ourselves.

When we are punished we have a sense of injustice that opens a wound in our mind. The wound creates emotional poison. We feel that pain in our heart as an emotional, not a physical, pain. From this wound ethereal poison seeps into our mind. Fear begins and starts controlling our behavior. We become afraid of being punished and we also fear not receiving a reward. The reward comes as a sign of acceptance. Domestication causes an internal struggle to be worthy of reward in others' eyes. Domestication becomes so strong that we no longer need anyone to domesticate us because we take over the task by punishing ourselves and occasionally rewarding ourselves.

Three components of our mind are actively engaged in self-domestication. First, the judge in our mind judges what we do. Second, the victim receives the judgment and usually the judge finds the victim guilty. The victim has a need to be punished. The third part of the mind involved is the belief system we have been taught which includes the rules on how to dream our lives. This belief system is a kind of constitution or holy book where everything that we believe without reflection is our truth. I call this belief system the Book of Hell. We can close this Book of Hell by asking to die to the old dream of the planet. We can leave hell as we begin to imagine ourselves in heaven on earth.

A young girl, eleven years of age, will soon have her first period and become a woman. There is a whole universe operating within the girl's body, including her organs, blood, nerves, brain and all communicative systems that operate between systems. When some of the organs in this young woman change, this information is known by the brain, which will push other organs to create certain kinds of hormones that complete the cycle. Ultimately the maturation process is controlled by the brain.

The maturation process of the woman is comparable to that of the human race as a whole. We can say that when the earth is mature enough it sends a message to the sun. The sun reacts and sends its message to trigger a change in humanity. When certain transformations of body, mind, and soul occur in some humans, the sun will change the quality of the light it transmits, sending a different message to the human organ of the earth. In turn, this change will cause the whole of humanity to transform.

Since the birth of the Sixth Sun humanity is finally ready to leave childhood and become mature. We are ready to leave domestication behind. We have more clarity. Our way of dreaming is changing. Fear was necessary to promote the growth of reason and the mind. Reason prepared the mind for intuition, a more direct connection to spirit.

spirit

THE FOUR PROPHECIES

According to the Toltec calendar—which is also the Mayan and Aztec calendar—there have been five suns prior to the one that exists now. These prophecies said that there would be a huge earthquake in Mexico's biggest city of Tenochtitlan. In 1986, this earthquake struck Mexico City, which is the modern Tenochtitlan. The ancient Toltecs predicted that after the earthquake there would be a five-year period of rest until the new sun was born. On January 11, 1992, the new sun came and it has sparked a great change in all humans.

PROPHECY ONE

Birth of the Sixth Sun

The birth of the Sixth Sun spawned an evolution of humanity. Our mind is changing. We are becoming aware that we are dreaming and that we are controlling our dream. Instinctively we are rejecting one quality of light and accepting another; as we do this, we are modifying our connection to the sun. We do not need to work for it to happen. It is occurring already. All modifications originate from the sun because it has supreme intelligence. Humans all over the world have recognized this. Ancient Egyptians worshiped Ra, the sun god. In Teotihuacan, they also knew that the sun controls the earth. They were aware that at certain intervals, life on this planet changed when the sun changed.

The Sixth Sun has a different quality of light and it is transforming the dream of Planet Earth. It will transform the human mind, making it more aware of itself as a light being connected to the sun. As an individuals, we will speed our own evolution if we just open to the new light, allow the light to flow freely inside of us and become who we really are.

The entrance of the Sixth Sun has changed me personally... I believed I had a special mission, a destiny, but the moment the light from the new sun entered, everything was gone. There was no mission. There was no man. There was no life. Inside I felt completely

full of joy, peace, and love. I no longer had to justify anything to myself or anyone else. The meaning of my work changed. I no longer felt I had a special gift to give others. I had thought I was God's worker, and he sent me for a reason. That is not truth anymore for me.

After this single day, I have seen the world with a different perception. I see it without judgment. The result is amazing. I'm not worried about the planet. I do not worry about nature. I do not worry about other people, war, a tornado, or someone shooting at me. I know that whatever happens has to happen. It is done as it should and I trust it one hundred percent.

I see a world with justice. We are already in a world of justice. In this new state of mind, I can see all the nightmares we have created in this world. It is easy to understand that emotional and physical suffering of humans comes from what we have created ourselves.

After that day, I could see myself as a two-year-old, playing all the time and having fun. When I was a two-year-old I couldn't see the world of injustice. I didn't know then that the way humans dream is a nightmare.

True bliss is to know *without* the innocence of childhood that this is a world of justice. We cannot remove the nightmare if we remain innocent as children. We must understand the dream of hell so we can get out of hell as soon as possible.

All the masters of earth are trying to tell us the same thing: we have something wonderful inside us and we can open to it. The mind is a living being. The mind eats and digests the emotions which come through ideas. As more and more masters speak of the silent knowledge, more and more humans will ingest these ideas.

This is the prophecy for the new humanity. *Human beings will know who they are.*

We are God

dreaming that

we are

not God.

Surrender. Whatever happens will happen because it must. Our task is to enjoy our life more and to express what is inside us to bring about the new humanity. If we have hate inside us, we share hate. If we have sadness, we share sadness. We can only share happiness when we are happy. We cannot share love unless we love ourselves first.

PROPHECY TWO

God awakens

The prophets said that when the Sixth Sun came, God would awaken from the dream. This means that we are God dreaming that we are not God. The day the dreamer awakes and becomes God is the same as resurrection. First, we have to become aware that we are asleep. Then we can awaken.

Although it will take at least two hundred years for this process of awakening to be completed, since 1992 the process has been accelerating and many of us have felt the effect in our lives. This is the generation that is beginning the awakening, and you are a part of it.

What we need to do is surrender. Whatever happens will happen because it must. Our task is to enjoy our life more and to express what is inside us to bring about the new humanity. If we have hate inside us, we share hate. If we have sadness, we share sadness. We can only share happiness when we are happy. We cannot share love unless we love ourselves first.

We don't understand why we suffer. We don't realize we have a choice, but we DO have a choice. We are not totally responsible for the old dream because it was here when we were born. In spite of the nightmarish dream, we are trying to make this a better place for our children. The Dream of the Planet has evolved through the millennia, so the dream is changing and

awaken

the tendency is toward something better, but for now it is still a nightmare, and it is still hell.

Our task in this lifetime is to extricate ourselves from the old dream. We cannot afford to wait for the new dream to evolve into fearlessness. We must act for ourselves.

The Dream of the Planet will not change without resistance, just as we cannot change our own dream without experiencing resistance. The beginning of a new dream is already here and it is growing, but the old dream wants to hang onto guilt, anger, the judge and the victim. The human pattern of spiritual growth is like an inner war where we face ourselves. We tend to be the most severe judge of ourselves.

Each of us will experience a crisis of surrender, but afterwards our capacity to love will increase. As it happens in the individual, it will also happen in all of humanity.

Expect there to be continuous temptations. Other living beings will try to tempt us back into the old dream by manipulation of our emotions. Jesus showed us how to resist temptation with love: You do not try to stop emotions of rage, you just allow them to flow through you.

All of our prophetic books describe the resistance of the Dream of the Planet during the time of change. The prediction of horrors relates to the fears released by resistance to change. During the last fifty years, the human race has tried to destroy itself from fear, but it has failed. Humanity has been in chaos, but the old dream is already broken and resistance is lessening.

In the *Revelation* in the Bible John speaks of the Seven Seals. At the time of his writing, letters were sealed with wax. It is symbolic that the seal had to be broken to read the information inside. Every seal that is broken in the book of *Revelation* increases our awareness of the modifications coming into the earth via light from the sun.

But there is no reason to fear the changes.

Even if our bodies die in some predicted disaster, we have no reason to fear. Our bodies will die anyway. Death is nothing but transformation. Do not listen to prophets of fear. Do not be guided by them. The old Dream of the Planet will try to preserve itself by creating fear.

Spirit is moving us to change our dream and the dream of the planet. When we entered the Sixth Sun, it gave us an opportunity to make this change in the dream. More than an opportunity, it was a command from the sun telling us it has to happen.

Intuition is going to

rule the next period.

Intuition is about

trusting. It is knowing

without thinking,

without doubt.

Once we are aware that we are directly connected to the sun, we can suggest a behavior to another of Earth's organs. Intuition connects us to our personal ray of light. This is why prayer is so powerful when we expect to have an answer.

PROPHECY THREE

Intuition guides our lives

There are three parts to the cyclic pattern of the dream of humanity. In part one, which is the darkest time, reason controls the dream. In the second stage, reason and intuition, are mixed. This leads to a fast period of growth and transformation. In the last stage, destruction of the old dream occurs in order to rebuild the dream. Today, we are almost at the end of that part of the cycle in which reason and intuition are mixed.

The next two hundred years will be a time of growth with the transformation moving faster and faster. There will then be a period of at least three or four thousand years of peace until a new cycle begins.

Intuition is going to rule the next period. Intuition is about trusting. It is knowing without thinking, without doubt. This is where we are in the cycle. Reason, which controls the false dream, has transformed now to intuition for those who are already changed.

We think we are the most intelligent species on Earth, but we are only a small piece of the universal intelligence. Ideas that we think are our own are really already in existence when we become aware of them and think that we "think" them. As we evolve, we will intuit ideas directly from where they are stored in nature.

Once we are aware that we are directly connected to the sun, we can suggest a behavior to another of

Earth's organs. This is the way that shamans control the rain. They do not do so with their *reason* but with their *intuition*. Shamans cannot connect with reason because reason always finds a reason not to believe in itself. Intuition connects us to our personal ray of light. This is why prayer is so powerful when we expect to have an answer. Usually, the answer to our prayer is not what the reason expects.

When we connect and witness in a shamanic way, it is not our personality that brings about changes. It is the sun. For the sun, everything is possible.

It is the same for each of us. We do not need to *expect* what happens. We do not need to *make* something happen. We ask and we witness. The sun, with its superior intelligence, will create the answer. How can we doubt our personal destiny? There is no place for doubts anymore.

Knowledge is a limitation, a barrier to freedom. Knowledge is only a description of the dream and what we dream is not real. So, knowledge is not real. Yet, knowledge seems valuable because we use it to communicate and interchange our ideas and our emotions. The problem is that if we put all the knowledge we have accumulated into our personal computer and base our actions on it, knowledge will prevent us from transcending its limitations.

Knowledge tries to convince our reason that transcendence is not possible. We need to cross the river of knowledge in order to transcend to intuition.

Our knowledge closes off our intuition. Intuition leads us to the truth. Truth is alive.

What will make the difference in the coming transformation is what is created in the mind. Far ahead of us, those we now call human will live in a different part of the universe. Those who remain here will have a new sort of energy. I do not think the humans of that time will have bodies like us. I believe they will live in the oceans. Today there are two species living in the oceans who are starting to dream as humans. The importance of the prophecies to us is that we are already transforming. We are already living a new dream. We are becoming new beings, new humans.

Love is the opposite of fear. Love is that fire that does not destroy, whereas fear is the fire that burns everything it touches.

Other people's love can awaken our love, but it is our own love that makes us happy. That love is our own truth. It is our freedom. That love will transform the old dream to the new dream of heaven on earth.

PROPHECY FOUR

Love creates heaven on earth

Love is creating the biggest transformation in the human world. For thousands of years humans have repressed love. We forgot what love means.

When we say "I need you," that is not love. That is possessiveness. If we feel jealousy and we want to control another that is not real love. Possessive love is like any other need of the human body. Imagine going without food for a week. You would feel as though you were starving. Then if someone gave you a taste of bread, you would feel, "I need this bread. I love this bread." Falling in love is something like that.

When we were four years of age, our emotional body was made of perceived love. Then, domestication began and fear began. Fear took the place of love. Every time we started to express our love, something in us repressed it. We felt hurt and we became afraid to love. We limited our love to just a few people. With others, we would say, "I love you, IF..." This meant, "I will love you if you let me control you." That love creates a strong dependency, just like a drug.

In a human relationship, one partner often has more need for love than the other partner and that partner gives power to the other. This is like the relationship between a drug addict and the supplier. The one who gives love is in complete control and can manipulate the other person through fear. A broken heart is like a drug addict who cannot secure the drug. It causes the same emotions. It is very common to be scared to love because for a small pleasure there is such a large payment.

love

During the last fifty years, marriage has changed so much that it has almost been destroyed. These changes had to happen as part of the process of cleansing and releasing all the emotions and fears present in relationships. Marriage will be recreated without the need to control another person. It will be based on respect. A woman will have the right to be one hundred percent herself. A man will have the right to be one hundred percent himself.

When we respect each other's dream, there is no conflict. When we are not afraid to love, when we do not stipulate conditions for our love, everything will change. Today, there is little respect. As soon as I tell you what to do, that means I do not respect you. Feeling sorry for someone shows a lack of respect. Feeling sorry is not compassionate. Feeling sorry for someone awakens your own self-pity. If I feel sorry for you, it means that I think you are not strong enough or intelligent enough to make it. If you feel sorry for me, you do not respect me or think that I am strong enough or intelligent enough to make it. Having compassion is seeing that someone has fallen, helping that person stand up, and then saying "yes" he or she can do it.

Even though we see people in the worst conditions, we do not need to feel sorry for them. We just need to witness and love them. We can help them with our compassion. A person can always choose a new dream.

Humans will recover their sense of responsibility. For centuries, we have tried to avoid responsibility, yet whatever we do always causes a reaction. We cannot escape cause and effect. We do not need to take responsibility for another's mistakes. We can help and give love, but we do not need to take responsibility for others because that encourages their illusion of avoiding responsibility. This applies even to our children, spouses, parents, or friends. If we take on their responsibilities, they become weak.

Our only responsibility in this life is to make ourselves happy. We do not need knowledge for that because everything we require is already here. Other people's love can awaken our love, but it is our own love that makes us happy. That love is truth. It is our freedom. That love will transform the old dream of hell to the new dream of heaven on earth.

The best way to take advantage of the change that is in process is to stop resisting it. We are not here to please others. We are here to please ourselves.

When we align our intent with love, we can do whatever we want. There is no doubt that we will become the person we were meant to be. This is true for everyone.

express your beauty

Action is what makes the difference in the new reality. The power is in the action, not in the dream. Through your actions, you have the power to change everything. You can claim the freedom to act on behalf of transformation and express your personal dream by creating a life filled with beauty and love.

As you begin to awaken to the new dream ask yourself, "How beautiful is my life? What is my intent? How much do I love? How happy am I?"

I encourage you to be the supreme artist of your personal dream and the dream of the planet. Make them as beautiful as possible. You are the light. You are love. Express your beauty with love.

*Thank you for reading my words and for
letting me love you as you truly are, a light being
connected to the sun by your personal ray of
sunlight, a being who is also God.
I love you.*

Don Miguel Ruiz

RETURN TO LIFE

I waken
And nothing is the same.
For the first time,
I open my eyes,
These eyes of mine
I long believed could see
And find that all I knew as true
Was nothing but a false dream.

The Angel of Life became
And transformed my dream
From a drama of fear
To a joyful comedy.

So surprised, I ask the Angel,
"Am I dead?"
She replies,
"Yes, for these many years,
Though your heart beat on,
Your mind slept in the grave of illusion
Unconscious of your divinity.

"Now, with heart beating
And body breathing,
Your mind has wakened from hell.
Renewed, your eyes
Admire the beauty awaiting you.

FEAR · LOVE ·
FEAR · LOVE · FEAR
VE · FEAR · LOVE ·
· FEAR · LOVE · F
· FEAR · LOVE · L
LOVE · FEAR · L
· FEAR · LOVE · F
R · LOVE · FEAR
VE · FEAR · LOVE
FEAR · LOVE · FEA
LOVE · FEAR · LO
EAR · LOVE · FEAR

"Your divine awareness wakens
All the love in your being.
Hating and fearing forsaken,
Gone are the guilt and the blame.
Your soul forgives,
Your divinity lives."

My eyes, in fascination,
Stare at the Angel.
Sensing the truth waking in me.
I surrender, willingly,
Without condition.
Humbly receiving
Death and life,
To hell, I release all claim
And with new eyes,
See my eternal love...leaving.

Miguel Angel Ruiz

REFLECTIONS

When the brain converts ethereal energy into words and writing, we manifest into the material world what we are dreaming in our mind.

being

dream

We are free to leave the nightmare and
dream heaven anytime.

light

Intent, spirit, God—these are names for the
same energy. Intent energy makes
possible any change, any transformation.

Humanity is finally ready to leave childhood and become mature. We are ready to leave domestication behind.

spirit

birth

We are becoming aware that we are
dreaming and that we are controlling
our dream.

awaken

We have to become aware that we are asleep.
Then we can awaken.

intuition

Intuition is about trusting. It is knowing without thinking, without doubt.

love

When we respect each other's dream,
there is no conflict.

WHAT IS THE SIXTH SUN FOUNDATION?

Thousands of years ago, the Toltecs were artists and scientists who formed a society to explore spiritual wisdom and practices in everyday life. The Toltec wisdom is brought into contemporary times through the guidance of don Miguel Ruiz, the author of *The Four Agreements*, *Beyond Fear*, and *Toltec Prophecies*. Sixth Sun Foundation is don Miguel's official non-profit organization that shares this wisdom in low-cost ways through Living The Four Agreements Wisdom Groups, Sixth Sun Membership Program and other partner programs.

The web address for the Sixth Sun Foundation is
www.sixthsunfoundation.org/sixthsunprograms.html

E · FEAR · LOVE ·
AR · LOVE · FEAR
VE · FEAR · LOVE
· FEAR · LOVE · F
E · FEAR · LOVE ·
· LOVE · FEAR · L
· FEAR · LOVE · F
R · LOVE · FEAR
VE · FEAR · LOVE
FEAR · LOVE · FEA
OVE · FEAR · LO
EAR · LOVE · FEAR